Amazing Salamanders

Written by Kerrie Shanahan

Flying Start
to Literacy®

Contents

Introduction

Salamanders are amazing animals. They look like lizards but they are not lizards. They have lived on Earth since the time of the dinosaurs and they still look the same as they did back then.

ancient salamander skeleton

Fact file

Scientists have found salamander fossils that are 160 million years old.

marbled salamander

There are many different types of salamanders. Some are smaller than your little finger and some are bigger than a person. Some live in caves, some in trees and some in water.

Salamanders have developed clever ways to survive. These include how they find food, how they keep safe and how they breed.

Chapter 1
What are salamanders?

Salamanders are amphibians, like frogs and toads. Most begin their life in water, then grow into air-breathing adults. Many salamanders go through incredible changes as they grow and become adults.

Fact file

There are about 500 species of salamander.

Salamanders have different colours and patterns on their skin. Some are brightly coloured with spots, stripes or other patterns. Salamanders that live underground are often plain white or pink.

tiger salamander

red salamander

ıbing salamander

7

The largest salamander is the Chinese giant salamander.   It can grow to about 1.8 metres long.

Salamanders vary a lot in size.   Most salamanders are about ten to twenty centimetres long.   The smallest salamander is less than 2.5 centimetres long, including the tail.

All salamanders breathe air to get oxygen into their bodies.   There are four different ways that salamanders do this.   Most salamanders use lungs to breathe.   Others that live in water have gills that they use to take in oxygen from the water.

Some salamanders, such as the blind salamander, have both lungs and gills. Most of the time they use their gills to breathe. When the amount of oxygen in the water is low, they use their lungs to breathe oxygen from the air.

Some salamanders do not have lungs or gills. They breathe in oxygen through their skin.

blind salamander

lungless salamander

9

Chapter 2
Where do salamanders live?

Salamanders are found in the USA, South America, Europe and Asia.

Most salamanders begin their lives in water and then live their adult lives on land. They live in and near marshes, swamps, lakes and creeks. They can be found under stones, on forest floors under damp leaves or in burrows.

fire salamander

Fact file

As salamanders grow, they shed a layer of skin. Then they eat this skin.

Salamanders need to live in a damp environment so their smooth, soft skin does not dry out. Salamanders help to keep their skin moist by making slimy mucus ooze out of glands in their skin.

11

Chapter 3

How do salamanders hunt?

Salamanders are carnivores – they eat other animals. They search for their food during the night and rest during the day. Animals that are active at night and rest during the day are called nocturnal animals.

Salamanders flick their tongues in and out rapidly to catch their prey. The prey gets stuck on the end of the salamander's sticky tongue. The salamander brings its tongue back in and eats the prey.

The giant palm salamander can flick out its tongue fifty times faster than the blink of an eye. Its tongue can extend nearly half the length of its body.

Fact file

Most salamanders eat insects, spiders, worms and snails. Some eat frogs, fish and even other salamanders.

The lungless salamander has an amazing way to hunt for food. It also uses its tongue to catch its prey, but it has developed a way to make this hunting technique even better.

This salamander's tongue is attached to a long bone. When the tongue shoots out of the salamander's mouth, the bone comes out behind it, extending the length of the tongue. This means the tongue can reach even further to grab prey.

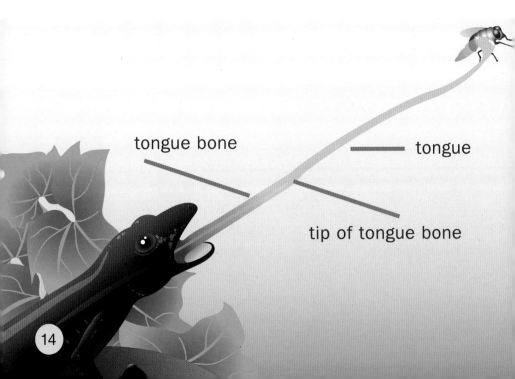

tongue bone

tongue

tip of tongue bone

lungless salamander

Fact file

One type of lungless salamander is about six centimetres long. Its tongue is five centimetres long.

When the salamander's tongue is fully extended, it is almost as long as the salamander's body.
When this salamander is not using its tongue to catch prey, the tongue is stored where the salamander's lungs would have been.

Chapter 4
How do salamanders stay safe?

Salamanders have some amazing ways to defend and protect themselves from predators that hunt and eat them.

Storks, snakes, owls and turtles are some of the animals that hunt and eat salamanders

Using poison

Many salamanders make poison to protect themselves from predators. Some salamanders have poison that comes out of glands in their skin. The poison has a bad taste so the predators that catch these salamanders will spit them out, keeping the salamanders safe.

The fire salamander sprays poison from glands along the middle of its back. The poison burns the eyes and mouth of a predator and can affect the animal's nervous system. Its muscles stop working and it cannot breathe.

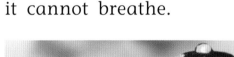

Fact file

Brightly coloured salamanders are often poisonous. The bright colours warn predators to stay away from them.

This spotted salamander is hard to see.

Hiding

Salamanders hide during the day. They hide from predators in underground holes or under leaves and bark.

Many salamanders can be hard to see because they are similar in colour to their environment. This helps to keep them safe from predators.

Tricky tails

A salamander can make its own tail fall off. It does this if its tail gets stuck or if it gets caught by a predator. After a salamander drops its tail, the tail keeps on wriggling. The predator is distracted and the salamander can escape.

After losing its tail, the salamander can grow a new tail.

Fact file

Salamanders can also regrow other body parts such as their legs and even their eyes.

This salamander is growing a new tail.

Chapter 5

How do salamanders grow and change?

Laying eggs

All salamanders lay their eggs in water. The eggs are covered in jelly and are attached to sticks or water plants. This helps to keep the eggs safe until they hatch.

Salamanders that live on land lay their eggs in water and leave their eggs to hatch by themselves. Salamanders that live in water look after their eggs until they hatch.

Fact file

Usually the mother looks after the eggs, but in some species, such as the Japanese giant salamander, the father looks after the eggs.

Hatching

After about four weeks the salamanders hatch out of the eggs. These salamanders are called salamander larvae. They look a bit like tadpoles. They have gills to breathe underwater, a long tail fin and no legs.

As soon as salamander larvae hatch, they are able to look after themselves. They use their strong tail fins to swim through the water hunting for food.

salamander larvae

salamander eggs

Growing and changing

Salamander larvae look very different from adult salamanders. To become adults, their bodies must go through incredible changes. This change is called metamorphosis.

Fact file

One type of salamander called the axolotl does not change as it grows into an adult. It stays in the larval state for its whole life. It uses its gills to breathe in water.

Metamorphosis begins when the salamander larvae are about three weeks old. First they grow front legs. Then they grow back legs. Then their tail fins become thickened tails.

Most salamanders develop lungs instead of gills and then move out of the water onto land. Their skin changes into its adult colouring.

Breeding

Each year most adult salamanders return to the pond or swamp where they hatched to mate and lay their eggs. For some salamanders this is easy because they live near where they hatched.

Fact file

The male salamander waves its tail in a kind of dance to show the female it is ready to mate.

This newt is laying its eggs on a tree root underwater. A newt is a type of salamander.

But other salamanders must travel a long way to do this. These types of salamanders use their strong sense of smell to find the exact place where they began their life. Once they get to the spot where they hatched, they find a mate and lay their eggs.

Salamander life cycle

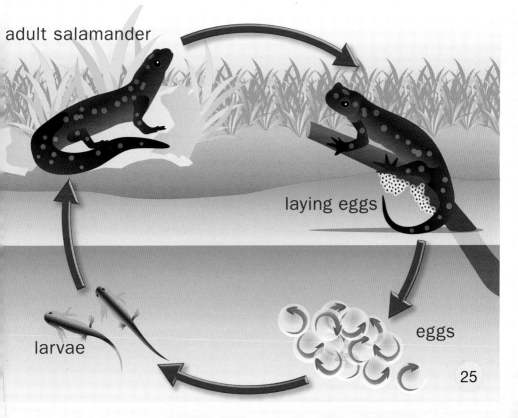

adult salamander

laying eggs

eggs

larvae

Conclusion

Salamanders are amazing animals. They have lived on Earth for millions of years and are found in many different countries. There are hundreds of different types of salamanders, all with their own unique look and behaviours.

Salamanders have developed characteristics that give them the best chance of survival. They have amazing ways of finding food and keeping safe from predators.

fire salamander

Glossary

amphibian A cold-blooded animal with smooth skin and a backbone that often lays its eggs in water.

gills Organs that let animals breathe underwater

gland An organ or cells that produce liquids in the body

larva A newly hatched animal whose body will go through many changes as it grows

metamorphosis The changing of an animal's body as it grows into an adult

nervous system The system of nerves in the body that carries messages to and from the brain

species A group of living things that are the same in many ways

A note from the author

To write this book about salamanders, I needed to find out information about them. As I researched salamanders, I kept discovering more and more incredible facts about these animals. I listened to David Attenborough, a well-known naturalist, talk about salamanders on a radio science show. I also looked at many, many websites on the Internet about salamanders.